W9-BAW-149

NERVES

NERVES

MIDDLEBURY COLLEGE
LIBRARY

John Wieners

Cape Goliard Press in Association
with Grossman Publishers New York

PS
3573
I35
N4
1970

8/1972
Serie

© copyright John Wieners 1970

This first edition was designed, printed and published by Cape Goliard Press, 10a Fairhazel Gardens, London NW6; of this edition 100 copies have been numbered and signed by the author.

Printed in Great Britain.

U.K. SBN 206 61976 6

U.S. SBNs paper 670 50605 2; cloth 670 50604 4
Library of Congress No. 76 127242

Some of these poems were previously published by: Anonym; The Frontier Press; The Iowa Review; Nine Queen Bees; The Journal of Creative Behavior; The Los Angeles Free Press; New College, Florida; Stonybrook 1/2; The Student Review; The Unicorn Press; The Western Gate; The Wivenhoe Park Review; The Perishable Press; The Paris Review; George Robert Minkoff; The Brownstone Press; Andrei Codrescu; The Institute of Further Studies; Noose; and Prologue.

The Asylum Poems were first published by Angel Hair Books, New York, 1969.

Photographs by Gerard Malanga.

SUPPLICATION

O poetry, visit this house often,
imbue my life with success,
leave me not alone,
give me a wife and home.

Take this curse off
of early death and drugs,
make me a friend among peers,
lend me love, and timeliness.

Return me to the men who teach
and above all, cure the
hurts of wanting the impossible
through this suspended vacuum.

1969

WITH MEANING

Rise, shining martyrs
over the multitudes
for the season of migration
between earth and heaven.

Rise shining martyrs
cut down in fire
and darkness,
speeding past light
straight through imagination's park.

In the smart lofts on West Newton St.
or the warehouse district of S.F., come,
let us go back
to bequeathed memory

of Columbus Ave., or the beach
at the end of Polk St.,
where Jack Spicer went,
or Steve Jonas' apts.
all over town

from Beacon Hill to St. Charles,
without warning how they went.
The multitude of martyrs,
staring out of

town houses now on Delaware Ave.
in the grey mist
of traffic circles, taking LSD
then not holding up
to rooming houses, Berkeley and motorycles.

Books of poems all we had
to bound the frustration
of leaving them behind
in Millbrook mornings, on the swing

with Tambimuttu, exercising his solar plexus
during conversation. Each street
contains its own time of
other decades, recollected
after the festival, carefully

as so many jewels
to brush aside for
present occupation.
A printing press by the Pacific,

a Norman cottage in the east,
dancing to Donovan, in Pucci pajamas,
or perhaps prison, past imagination's plain,
with Saturday night sessions in the tombs, oh yes
rise shining martyrs, out of the movie house's matinee

on Long Island, to your love walking by
in the sun. Over the multitudes,
shortripping. And backyard swimming pools
of Arizona or Pacific Palisades,

in the canyons of L.A.
plus the journeys over oceans
and islands, to metropolis
spreadeagled the earth.
Yes rise shining martyrs

out of your graves, tell us
what to do, read your poems
under springtime moonlight.
Rise and salvage our century.

CASUAL LOVE

causal, gives to her, joy
in the chair, sitting naked
looking at her lover,
asleep in bed.

Casual love, so easy to get,
so hard to forget yet
casual arms around a
casual waist

with marijuana regret
nothing, long hours passed
in love, he will not come
her way again. He's gone

to work by dawn. Deep waves carry him
out to sea, where one may not see
beyond his brown body / nothing.
Old rain falls on the windowpane.

Two o'clock rolls round again,
any two o'clock. Sinatra sings on the radio
It Had to Be You. Naked in the chair
Georgia On My Mind, listening

as moonlight, clear and sweet
through the pines. He will be gone
another naked dawn, another man
left out of her life.

2

She just picked him up or
rather he passed her by
on the street, turned around and
she took him home in a taxi, stopping

on the way to buy a fifth of whiskey.
She could not resist, what matter
he was black, drawn as she was, he has
not come yet, she thought suddenly,

I hope I dont have to go through that again.
Sitting up in the chair, a bed only big enough for one.
I wont get no sleep
dim music started to play.

She did not care, as saxophone and smoke began to blare,
through a trombone for riches and kings.
These were not her things
only marijuana and she meant it,

Stella By Starlight crept over the machine
and imagining a white leather pump
slung around her ankle,
she did not care again.

1965

QUEER

Do I have to accept his
repetition of rival thrust
use of assholes and bitches
to gain entry of a youth's kiss?

run by alcoholics and fakes
to penetrate each night
with the tenderness and pride
from ambition's sneer.

1967

BILLIE

He was as a god,
stepped out of eternal dream
along the boardwalk.

He looked at my girl,
a dream to herself and
that was the end of them.

They disappeared beside the sea
at Revere Beach as
I aint seen them since.

If you find anyone
answering their description
please let me know. I need them

to carry the weight of my life
The old gods are gone. What lives on
in my heart

is their flesh
like a wound,
a tomb, a bomb.

1966

HOW TO COPE WITH THIS?

A mean, dark man
was my lover
in a mean dark room
for an evening

till dawn came
we hugged and kissed
ever since, first and last
I have missed

him, his mean, dark ways.
Mean, dark days
are upon me in the sunlight
even yet, I fear his foot

feel his cock and know it
as my own, my sown
seeds to reap
when the full neap

of pleasure falls, his kiss
reminds me, our dance
in the dark, my hope
and only scope.

1968

THE SUCK

This morning
last evening, yes
terday afternoon

     in the hall
your voice, full
of complement

turns to strike
someone you do not

know as a wife or brother,

shaking, trembling
in your arms
sweating like seventeen

again under young middle-aged

bellies in the summer.

1968

LOOKING FOR WOMEN

to serve me cookies and lemonade
       in the afternoon
with strains of destroyed music
under elms of a formal path.
Wanted a linen panama and ice-cream
       chair
Round table rusted from a sudden
       shower
Dripping umbrella over
       youth's terrace.

1968

STROLL

There are no men
for what else then
are they forgotten

or regretted even
surely no barren Eden
replaces that heaven,

or woman, her
trousered November
does little to cover

the final reminder
of honest desire
embodied under

innocent mien.

1969

CONCENTRATION

I'd half-expect
you were there
when I turned around
if I had courage to
accept that fact you're not.

In a bus station
listening to voices
pretending they're yours.
Poetry is a trance
of make-believe.

Dreaming morning
away like the time
we were in the country
when you threw me out
early for no reason.

How I cried?
I went to bed and dreamt
for years you were mine
beside me as you still are —
guide, guardian, friend.

Your laughter
mocks and derides
as supposed to,
a door slamming shut
on a locker locket

Miles away
I never see you
though am sick at
that thought
writing in light

without you. This dream
improves with time, as
you clear your throat or
tiny footsteps on the floor
herald another absence.

Other humans seem alien
to your presence, they're believed to,
it's a condition of gradual loss
of reality until there's only left
this shattering of the world.

1970

W W

A freshness in the dusk,
lilies of the valley easter on
Park Avenue, one day

visitors from Hudson country shop
at Byrnes and Marthe's,
a handkerchief's reprieve

choking ghosts of vanished authors
refresh first well-placed wives
in travail of fleeing manners,

a task beyond ennui
Two splits of casino libation husband
retrieve one midnight essex.

1967

I'M

pretending with him
accustomed to absence
his breath filled rooms

that afternoon gone as snow
we stepped through before tea and sandwiches,
photographs, a letter —

in the garage talked
his thighs full, calves so tawny
driving two hundred miles

the day after
Thanksgiving, it was
following

late supper and champagne
we drove back by
this house parking —

lot talk of a poem, the figure
of one friend remains
perhaps to kiss again.

1967

DOT

my divorced aunt's
flatfoot checks
her dead husband's
peter

in a locker
John
questions that
dirge

    her tea's
    been wait-
    ing since
    seepin

bitter snipe
to cheek
mate's
throttle.

1968

INSULTED

I never rewarded, never cared
why didn't I
when they burnt your head

saw you beat mother instead
after you're dead
suspended

in what you shouldn't
despite one-eyed poison
from the woodshed

had to look upward
or under black polished stove
his dreaded tread,

marks of the rapist,
fed teacher coal shovel
flames of hatred

in bed that noon
heard shredded thread
of parentage divided.

Not David, was it?
no it isn't, heavy handed
she said, derided

what I didn't hear,
that spring Czecho-
slovakian spread folded,

bled all over the floor included
I fled for the door,
who needs that old maid

I didn't care, I wouldn't

OSTERREICH

The man I'm kissing
lives right here
despite all odds

on my lips,
heals parchment desire
allows old streets' flow,

his whispers my wound,
condemnation the only gesture
allowed him to know.

offing me to others, who
stab my side to death
with stakes and threats.

1967

TOURS

The middle-aged lovers belie
their wives and husbands
to enter that damned estate

of stone lions and watery lawns in the arboretum
forgoing limbs of habit and home
to parade stolen flesh pouched inside

bellies, low-slung from domestication
and diviation. Ungrateful rejects
of the hearth, jackal and pig poke

as antiquaries over spirited relics
spread before crossed or single sword
in delayed romance. Swains on summer holiday

dress imported style, terry-clothed terriers
and Ecuador chapeaux board-walk
la haute.ville for bypassed boyhoods—

misbegotten eavesdropping earnest energies
fill mother's album with monotone newsreels
naked in languishing insult, the

nervous insistence of neighbors and newspapers
drives them back by autumn to write
documentary diaries, decoded distresses

from another dire Deauville, another distinct duel
with that devil in the sun, dissolved by tears
at the seashore, or in the room, alone at home.

May 17, 1968

A DAWN COCKTAIL

We lie in a pool of blood,
smashed glass all over stone
cut neck, chest, calves
bleeding to death
over moonlit goblets.

MENU

Cranberry steak
and blueberry champagne
take the bitter out,

a hollow cock
beats goose hands
around some pheasant

shepherd's lamb
in my mouth
throbbing signals

de la fete,
calves brains
with Marino wine.

1968

TO DO

Forgotten what once loved
early death, the loneliness
of summer afternoons on apple boughs

down past brook field uptown
before parched adolescent love
dirty boys together by a stream

surprised caretakers in what they do
climbing over dams behind
blind pebbles lane, under bushes

first come, first served forgetting
world renascence at their feet,
yearning to be caught, held and

told in crushes' obedient trust.

1969

KEEP IT

Your mind's path
is an alien
street corner
at Columbus and Grant Avenue, its
desire sordid a
park at dawn
littered with newspaper
and toilets,

        perhaps
92nd Street and West End
after benzedrine flattered
the attention.

Persistent as a question
already asked of
sweetness unshared,

vulgar noise heard
in the hall or
woman's hand with a whip
across the neck.

1967

NAKED

An old man and a woman
came to torment me
in the desert with ants
and honey.

Three children set me free
marching proudly over the
clearing, tearing bands
of meat

from my arms, leaving
me empty to meet my love.
Who was waiting in bed
for me.

PIAZZA

throw keys down
to a man in the square
reading papers by sunlight

well-built, immune to flattery
who holds his own so long
outside the park

forbidden entrance, no matter
how often he slides
denied quiet interruption, the strength

of single gesture lost
twin alloy to true counsel
man's fault returns original habit.

UNHIRED

You can't do him
he doesn't have it
that way, tonight
you can't hear
him, half-blind

that's an only way
he gets by, he had
a down blond kid
with him behind
dark glasses

on hot baths for months
under a celling fan
off Times Square
shades drawn in
to cheap insult's glare.

1968

NO LOVING SON

Stretch his brains on the rack
take the pus out, breathe
foetid odor's
taunted deprivation

grave concern what you mean
when you say
death uttered no threat
in tortured remembrance

's accusation fails adoration
your blind hatred
runs obviously
a theft

hurled against stone walls
of ingratitude practiced
over your head
in solitude.

1967

IN PUBLIC

Promise you wont forget
each time we met
we kept our clothes on
despite obvious intentions
to take them off,
seldom kissed or even slept,
talked to spend desire,
worn exhausted from regret.

Continue our relationship apart
under surveillance, torture, persecuted
confinement's theft; no must or sudden blows
when embodied spirits mingled
despite fall's knock
we rode the great divide
of falsehood, hunger and last year

1968

PAUL II

The faces of children
encourage deeds
of innocence

to take up arms
against eastern
indulgence

forced from slumber
to admit the falsehood
of goodness age reveals.

1966

WEDNESDAY OR SOMETHING

I might even listen
to what he did
to you in bed

up to your knees, just
home for the holidays
a basket off-shore,

mixed-up, naked to
desire gone before
he arrived

dated, undressed and
double-crossed,
Tuesday's rebellion.

DESPERATION

In what mad pursuit, or competition
the marvelous denies object
to what subject melancholy resignation?

drowned exile flight
down what exit, fall's fused endeavor
discharges incessant order

for what crushed languor,
what hapless ascension
rejected entreaties pace

cruel chase, within vain decline?
Annoyed, over-drawn, exempt
to what rest, borrowed dichotomy

unmasks its single purpose.

1968

SILVER RINGS

It seems as eternity
might get a hold on it,

some design numerical
determined our birth
preordained love

unmarried overfed
what happened when
your stomach turned over

my face hardened, bloated
from desire unsatisfied

still filled
at bitterness and rage

with such frustration
one day, one hour together
in a room, a motel

would be enough
shades drawn to violet dawn
fields soaking wet.

ACCEPTANCE

Should I wear a shadowed eye,
    grow moustaches
delineate my chin

accept spit as offering,
    attach a silver earring
grease my hair

give orders to legions
    of lovers to maintain manhood
scimitars away as souvenirs?

Sooush, beloved! here is my tongue.

INDIGNATION

It doesn't matter if one lives or dies
without desire. I tried to go away
on my own. Instead came back home

defeated to more defeat, worse
that it was met by discord
of an hideous sort, cursing and swearing

from a lower class of orders, dying at the doorstep.

All the men I wanted were married to others
and poetry in my heart burned
out. Left at afternoon ill,

what I approached
was to fall dead by my own hand
or close to it, nervous, afraid to move

I cannot blame them, only the men I wanted
are not here anymore, still the possible
freedom of their love is my dream.

1970

APPARITION

I feel his hands upon me
even tho he's not here
they draw me in to kiss.

Am I on the right way
or do I miss
what else may dreaming lead to

if it's not more bliss.
Perhaps I should quit
if this is not it.

Even when he comes close
I wont go there
what labor to explain

what's a bore to begin with
a sad and lonely dream
worse if come true.

CONSOLATION

Waiting at the window
in winter
for some trace of spring?

or any figure
to ease incoherent
blindness from absence.

There's one tree out there
with still a patch of snow
on its trunk

and a cat in the yard
though birds are missing
for days due to storm.

It's best not to think too much.
What awaits but death?
A long life of misery.

As branches bend in wind
We accept this futility
looking for love

Knowing we never will find same.
What to do but grow
away from the sun

Unless to think on the past
a vapor that escapes
from the mind in impatience

Best to get away from one's self
one's own life
for it leads to frustration

no matter who one is,
or what he has done.
The loneliness of hotels linger

in grey mid-Manhatten
in mid-morning mist
as taxis splash through rain.

1970

DEPRIVATION

Roses, lilacs and rains
over smell of earth, freshly
turned Saturday morning for
lovers' walks down strange lanes.

Never again recaptured
never again to find, oh how
our mind rebels at this, never
again to kiss that girl

with ameythst eyes, or watch
sunrise over the harbor, never again
to visit the grape arbor of childhood,
or remove the memory stain

of these events from our firm, budding youth,
mad truth of these trysts to lose
in time their hidden passion & meaning.

FEMININE SOLILOQUY

If my dreams were lost in time
as books and clothes,
my mind also went down the line
and infused with other longing

of a desperate sort, a sexual kind
of nightmare developed where every breath was
aimed at another man, who did not know
it, until I informed him by letter

And said nothing. As delusions lift off
I see I paid an ultimate price
and left in loneliness, nervous shaking
wracks day and night with residue.

It's impossible to make clear.
I wanted something, someone
I could not have, until I began
to sound like him, imitate him

at his shy insistence from a distance.
A Venice where floods of onanism took hold.
This self-indulgence has not left me.
Normal relations seem mild.

I am drowsy and half-awake to the world
from which all things flow.
I see it as gowing old
if only the price paid were not so great,

And what I wanted wanted me.
But it cannot be.
I wished these things since I was twelve
and the more impossible, or resistant

to the need, the deeper hold they had on me.

LOVE-LIFE

Chains are a terrible thing to wear
Unless of one's own making
Even terrible to bear.

More fierce cunning of the mind
That invents its own breaking
To seek then resort to blind —

Oh, who's choosing this kind
Hopeful burden to share
Without recourse by party or at fair.

Aforesaid hope may release the pair
But as it is, one sees no desert
Of challenge or care; to go on this way

Unsatisfied yet near the raking
Naked to love's own sword or sorry speech
Each to each unto death soothe the caking

Perhaps shake the partner by force
But on what course to proceed, rhyme less
Confined continuing the committment

By one's words condemned
To love this person, no matter what slaking
On taking of curse off by proximity

Still that anger hurts, this agony apart.
How to share our burden together.

Though the gift has gone.
The handwriting changed.
And the mind broken in two.
By such aimless arrow.

Of lust, of must
of past sex lingered.

1969

INOPERABLE

A chair of frustrated ambition
piled with yesterday's papers
in an unpaid room draws

haphazard mementoes' heedless
acquisition, an ivory cigarette holder,
scarves from Paris, stolen necklaces,

orphan gifts from another dynasty,
scotch jiggers a propped-open window,

the final film to passion's desertion.

READING IN BED

by evening light, at the window, where wind blows
it's not enough to wake with morning
as a child, the insistent urge of habit

sounds, to write a poem, to pore over one's past
recall ultimate orders one has since doubted
in despair. Inner reality returns

of moonlight over water at Gloucester, as
fine a harbor as the Adriatic, Charles said, before the
                                             big storm
blew up to land ancient moorings, shards against sand

of memory at midnight; ah yes the dream begins
of lips pressed against yours over waves, tides,
hour-long auto rides into dawn, when time

pounds a mystery on the beach, to no death out of reach.

January 9, 1970

ON THE BACK TO THE COVER OF
THE ALGERIA POEMS

This loneliness more than I may bear
gazing at the river
this loneliness with all of life
hearing waves lap on shore

what happiness is there
what's in store
as sun sets along Charles
lovers stroll the overpass,

gulls hawk their final farewell to day,
and I rise to go
to meet some one along the quai who
might dispell this awkwardness

if they were there.

I have sat here so often
in nervous trembling
this might be found out, with
a thousand pills in my stomach

afraid to be robbed
unable to sleep
on and on
for years.

REALIZATION

Where has that old spark gone
this sickness could come on?
What use in pretending
our dream of love undone

Old farms await to take us in
to their disease
under rotting apple trees

Going from one drugstore to the next
in snow, as there were someone
to dream of, these things not so,

but left alone, with mother
that is always lonely, to deny all dreams —
the penance of middle age.

DETERMINATION

Poetry is some way
of keeping in touch,
something to do
against staring at the wall, blankly.
It's some way
of filling loneliness
without politics.

Ceasing endless cruising
unclean hands, making
an effort where one doesn't have to.
Activity of one's own,
much as Mother's bedroom
or twilight, Sunday evening
when one's parents feel old.

PATRICIANS

The race belongs to the strong
The race belongs to death
Death is strong, death is the race.

ASYLUM POEMS

(For my Father)

1 9 6 9

THE DARK BREW

for Louise

At least these wounds were opened
by your love that allowed the deeper sickness in,
yea, they budded lush and festival in the dark
Silence of summer agony; when supposed love wreathed on the hill
these dark lilies grew beneath and polluted the stem

So two or three years later, I collapse under the burden,
the dark love grew immense in another's form
And silenced all holocust in their wake.
Belladonna of morning, autumn grapes for symphony and pansy
Immediately following as birth in place of life of foetid mind
Why go on; the list is endless what these wounds
                    your love opened, fed.

First hallucination of transient loveliness; second, voices of
self-importance, guiding and cajoling, cancelling all
connection to nature; third false vision of love and
its simples; fourth murderous challenge to the
dawn of thought, and envy, jealousy, rage as
accompaniments to artistry.

Some women bathe their hands in these blossoms,
and wear them pinned to their brows, as stars; others
anoint their bodies with the petals, calling a cape of
it perfume and pay enormous prices for its
scent, pollen caught off any extreme as death
but the chaos, culmination, conflagration of
what should be love's union but is not is
simply pest of confusion in the face of order.

What odor called forth by these buds, spring rain under murderous taxi tires,
a store window open to new design; the fresh arousing of debutantes on
                                                      Madison Ave.?
Who knows the stop signals of their gas, their lightning roar from cliffs on
                                                      country roads,
the damp spring we allowed to forget; why stop; the abandoned goats milk
                                                      from Pennsylvania
Ah there the haven lies in some sweet vision of your collapsing purple
                                                      amethyst eyes?
      within a face not mine to surmise, ringed with outshooting apple
                                                      blossoms.
Oh, who knows the look of false surprise; the badgering pity
the dream of death lives still under morning's sunrise,
despite the clatter of broken bumper and shining festoon
of afternoon's patience for drank twilight to halo drawn's root cart.
there where I was splattered, now taken in its guise
on field and bed, as one wounded must arise
these dark bruises regard as love defended.

ESPIONAGE

I sit in the evening, not on it
this time the back porch of a building, designed in 1933,
the year when conceived, enjoying clear twilight breeze.
Finished a bottle of coke, and my last cigarette, before retiring,
a blind man stumbles out, tapping his cane loudly.

6.28.69

SUISSE

Mountain'd nature is also an enemy
in that it wipes out identity.

Winters are less so
witness my chalet *au vierge*

at least malificent are more mani-
fest before the hounds of spring

mean nothing, next to it,
the dexterous elements of spring

sound alike, bird; robin, who dunnit?
While winter comes on like a bride,

in night gown, robeing the town.
What about spring, or summer then.

Summer is a communion, don't forget it,
Be a poet to handle it.

                The autumn lakes ablaze,
                        with brown
        leaves from summer's ashes. And winter again

        Carries autumn out
its lakes gone dry, barren, fertile fields went sour

for what, the dour memory of
wheat fields' gathered harvest.

6.30.69

SUSTENANCE

Your letters and my answer
sleep in a book of poetry;

no often how plenty,
are sure company.

What anacrostic daydreams
disturb this deepest pit

searching at one time for melancholiac act;
fell victims to depression

that cheer me up. They do not stink
no instance how filled with pieties.

Verities of adolescence, proven substance
by companions through childhood,

nightmare's misery
no matter how lost, twisted and illegible

Contorted and painful truth.

TRIMETERS

Your lips in a cloud
the spirit that visited
before I died
still assigned to the dead

the cyanide garments
that spirit vented
with tears in payment
from provincial rent

Without personal burden
only refuge denied
such taking allowed
as federal government

6.27.69

FORTHCOMING

to Fernand Leger

I died in loneliness
for no one cared for me enough
to become a woman for them
that was not my only thought
and with a woman
she wanted another one

I died in loneliness
of that I am not afraid
but that I am a clank
upon the gutter, a new guard at twilight
without a dream of adolescence
frustration plucked as strong

I died in loneliness
without friends or money
they were taken off
long ago, a melodrama
sounded out my name, the glass key of a
torch song on Father's Day

I died in loneliness
away from the beach and speeding cars
back seat in love with Bunny
on the way to Howard Johnson's
beyond the blue horizon
hunting for a lost popular tune.

6. 22. 69

THE PATIO

I created eternity
to bind you within it
A scheme worthy of the pope
to keep my prince

An ivory wall, have you seen it? there
as we travel on the road, together'd
shadows flit at twilight
we will not be one of them vespers

failing in confinement.
I built it. Where are you?

6.22.69

HIGH NOON

15 years of loving
men, women and children
with what result

Another silver Iseult
joins svelte Tristan
down a vault of tears

under what insult
account with drawn
on sorrow's bank

to sit up straight
at a stranger's voice
while he whispers miles away,

over the ocean at Cornwall
Brest, Dieppe land of melancholy
how surely these years wash away.

Gold Iseult comes to tarnish
Sylvan Tristan speeds in a white Falconetti
nude under afternoon sun

one dark haired lover on his mind
a man, not a woman inspires generations ahead
before dead legions arise

6.20.69

PRIVATE ESTATE

Dancing dandelions
and buttercups in the grass
remind me of other summer
flowers, simple blossoms

roses and tiger lilies by the wall
milk pod, sumac branches
lilacs across the road, daisies, blueberries
snaps, cut violets

three years ago still grow in my mind
as peonies or planted geraniums, bachelor buttons
in downy fields filled with clover
lover, come again and again up fern

path upheld as memory's perennial
against stern hard-faced officers of imprisonment
and cold regulation more painful than lover's arms
or flowers charming but not more lasting.

No, the wild tulip shall outlast the prison wall
no matter what grows within.

6.21.69

STOP WATCH

     the sensation
1)   of 10 assorted dancers
     in a crowded dining room

     moving as one person
2)   in unison
     to a popular tune

     during late afternoon
3)   hip and thighs beat
     with sparkling feet

     over the stucco floor
4)   before an open door
     how fortunate, how poor

     we were without the sign,
5)   symbol of recurrence
     or occurence

     surrounded
6)   by buff walls
     it was not a waltz

     only a standard rock
7)   song, much as students
     speak in rejoinder

     to a classroom; the same decibels
8)   happened in a bookstore when I rose
     using the newspaper I had as a fan;

the leaves of clover
9)   fluttering these three
unities I have known

as a tone to a bell's
10) gong, none of them
lasting longer

than 10-12 seconds
11) pressing history, light
in memory reckoned.

6.20.69

and the thought that a great love
affair might be awaiting still
spurs one on to imagine its
final ultimate surrender
    In the dark of the night,
under the linden branches of
a small New England academe,
to submit with one great cry
at the blind abused intrusion
of a god or king.
                To side-kick
docilely, in trust as possibly
that could be the one, whose
own experience so excited
you, there could be no choice
of course in love, before
  as Mabel Mercer
through rainy evenings, submerged

devoured memories of 21 in Back Bay
amoureuse avec la nuit, amoureux avec le printemps
en amour avec l'homme de style, speeding around

Plaza parking lots, horribly, madly, as the French might say
without means, over dreams, losing above one's beams.

6.18.69

MORGANA LA FAY

The return of
again is it
love we look, not
nearly so, only

the absolute inde-
prudence of youth, in
expectation, despite
Charles Dickens.

The first time going to the museum
alone, on to the library
walking Newbury Street after
the rain, and dining out,

visiting New York City on the late evening
trains. These things she thought
as the rain pelted the
trees on Long Island during the day,

and bumped into F. Scott
Fitzgerald, how he lived still
and his Long Island, always the place
to return, trembling alone

his and Zelda's Babylon
at Christmas, now living in a motel, this evocation
contained in the embrace of phantom love, and
to slip a peg, Lester Young by Times Square

6.19.69

JUST AN ORDINARY JOE

with plain face and wrinkled forehead
superabundant in his plaints and desire,
loving one with great passion,

now on guardian's gate, forlorn, fertile
and fruitful, the little doll, how he could love
her, *so my arms ache to talk of it, the reason*

why I stay away, alone in money's prison.
The heiress' call unheard except by an impossible
man who could help her, locked interruption to

funds, social register, impotent in battle.
A true Beckett of passion brooding o'er psyche.
How to decipher their distress thus accomplish plot.

Of ancient rich girl aiding tarnished knight *en armour.*

6.30.69

TIMES SQUARE

a furtive queen
hurrying across a deserted thoroughfare
at dawn.

AU NATURAL

An handsome man has to think a certain way.
Honest, courageous and brave

He would be a knave
to think a different way

Another should be true, loyal and good.
He looks like he would

Come to your aid, if need be
Despite a certain look of sleazy

Appearance, his disappearance would be apt
And opportune, happy

And in tune to another man's needs,
Be it pumpkin, water or seeds.

He would come to good deeds,
Of that you can be sure —
                              Naturally.

MELANCHOLY

Across the deep and brine
we'll go, Tristan and his lass, a ho,

up the meadow, away from men,
hand in hand, we'll lie down again.

Dark hair streaming to the wind,
Inhaling life as if our kin,

oh Tristan and his lass we'll go,
up the brine, down the glen.

Hand in hand, over men
And glad to see one another again,

sturdy lass I'll be for there,
and faint-hearted song you'll whisper.

REMOVED PLACE

When the echo falls
one will dismiss it.
When it calls again,
one will miss
it, falling in love with the present,
while one is able of it.
When the shadows enlarge, will one
enter it, or stay where
he is now. What will one do, how

AFTER SYMOND'S *VENICE*

for Allen Ginsberg

Boston, sooty in memory, alive with a
thousand murky dreams of adolescence
still calls to youth; the wide streets, chimney tops over
Charles River's broad sweep to seahood buoy; the harbor
With dreams, too; *The Newport News has arrived for a week's stay*
Alan, on Summer Street sailors yet stride along summer afternoons

and the gossamer twilights on Boston Common, and Arlington Street
adrift in the mind, beside the mighty facade of convent and charnel house,
who go through those doors, up from Beacon Street, past the marooned
                                         sunset in the
West, behind Tremont Hill's shabby haunts of artists
and the new Government Center, supplanting Scollay Square.

Who replace the all night films; and the Boston dawn
in the South End, newly washed pavements, by night's horses.

What happens here from the windows on Columbus Avenue
to Copley Plaza, and the library, Renaissance model, the Hotel and smart
                                         shops down
Newbury Street's lit boutique, lept by Emerson College,
who triumph light over dark, the water side
endures beside the moon and stars of Cambridge's towers

. . . past Park Square payements so wide for the browser, drifters
from Northampton Street behind the Statler, by the bus stations and slum
                                         tableaux
Finally to return to the Gardens, and the statue of George Washington
appealing to later-day shoppers to go home, in what dusk
what drunken revelling matches this reverie
of souvenirs, abandoned in the horror of public elevators

as this city is contained time, and time again the State House
from Bullfinch's pen, over School Street and Broad
        down the slope of Federal mirages over blue grass
to the waterfront; Atheneum holding all the books of men, directed
against the foe, hapless Pierre churns through the Parker House
        coming to the Vendome mentally
over the Brunswick, eternal in the mind's owl
        of phantoms stretching from boyhood.

When vows first establisht were to see this world and part
        all within it
You, Boston, were the first, as later San Francisco, and before that
New York, the South and West
penetrated, hard holds the Northwest, Chicago, Detroit
much in the same manner of industrial complexes
covering the rising cigarettes of patriots.

The Park Street Steeple as painted by Arshile Gorky zooms higher.
Slumbering city, what makes men think you sleep,
but breathe, what chants or paens needed at this end, except
you stand as first town, first bank of hopes, first envisioned paradise
by the tulips in the Public gargoyle's crotch, Haymarket
Square included spartan business enterprise and
next to South Station, the Essex evoking
        the metropolitan arena hopes entertain.

August 25, 1969